You Bet Your Laugh

A Concoction of Cartoons

IRON FROG
PRODUCTIONS
ironfrog.com

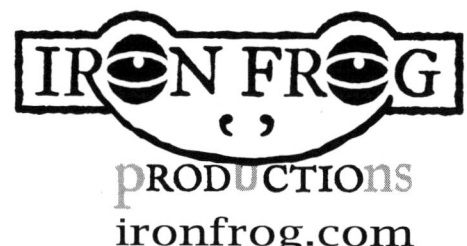

Dedication

This book is dedicated with love to the memory of my wife and childhood sweetheart, Ruth. We were together for 42 beautiful years. She was my treasured partner at both home and at work. My family and I miss her very much. She was a wonderful mother to our children, Gary, Craig, and Jay. She did a great job raising all four boys! As my mother used to say, "God bless that Ruth."

———————————————

In addition, I dedicate this book to my lifelong best friend, Mike Cloud and his loving wife, Linda. I met Mike in the first grade at St. Patrick's Grammar School in Jersey City, New Jersey. Mike passed away in November, 2018.

Acknowledgments

Love and special thanks to my three sons for all their help in creating this book—Gary, for his excellent guidance as copy editor, proofreader, and general advisor; Craig, for his superb work as book designer; and Jay, for his great job as financial advisor for the project. I'm very proud of the men they have become and am thankful for the support and encouragement they have provided to bring this book to life.

Thanks to Martha Scanlon Hackney, who helped me select which cartoons to include in the book. We reconnected recently after not having seen each other since we were classmates in high school sixty years ago.

The artwork in this book was created by Sandra Elliott and Penny Litts in association with Caricatures by Characters in Kissimmee, Florida. Sandra and Penny are sisters who have drawn together since they were children. Their brother, Thomas Elliott, Jr. contributed his talents to this project as well. Thanks to all three of them for drawing on their talents and these pages.

Foreword

My two favorite punsters in the world share the same names. One is Julius Henry Marx, better known as Groucho. The other is Julius Henry Roma, my Dad. (A curious coincidence: Groucho's first wife's name was Ruth—as was my Mom's.)

I was raised on a continuous stream of puns from both Julius Henrys. My father and I regularly watched Marx Brothers' movies together as well as reruns of *You Bet Your Life*, Groucho's television quiz show. More importantly, I was lucky enough to sit next to the Wordplay Wizard himself at the dinner table every evening. The question my Dad regularly asked my brothers and me after we took our first bites was, "Is it good, men?" We had learned from an early age that the proper response to that question was a robust, "Benny!" (For those too young to remember, Benny Goodman was a jazz clarinetist and big bandleader.) One time after supper when I was in elementary school, my Dad reviewed my homework and took issue with my answer to the question, "Is it the former or the latter?" He told me it must be the former because the latter was in the garage. I still remember my teacher groaning when I passed the pun along to her the following day.

When I started performing standup comedy, I dished out a routine cooked up entirely of puns. My template was full in the form of my father. (As I'm certain my Mom would contend, it was a template in need of a good scraping and scrubbing!) The steady diet of puns my Dad fed me while I was a growing boy served me well. I am grateful my father is a gourmet kook—I mean, cook!

Well, I suppose I should wrap this up "just in the nicotine," as my Dad says, before I drag on for too long. I am proud of my Dad and feel very fortunate to be a chap of the old bloke. Without father ado, do enjoy his book!

Gary Roma

Introduction

I have found some things echo over the hills and valleys of the years. When I was in high school, I wrote an essay about Henry David Thoreau in which I included some of my own humor. My teacher, Ms. Elizabeth Muller, asked me to read my paper in front of the class and then complimented me on my sense of humor. Those few, kind words have stayed with me. When I had to decide a couple years later what to study in college, I already had an interest in advertising and marketing, but Ms. Muller's words came to mind and I felt I could put my wit to good use in those fields.

Another echo from that time that continues to resound all these years later is my first date with my then-future wife, Ruth. On Friday, October 18th, 1957, we went to see *Tammy and the Bachelor* starring Debbie Reynolds at the Roosevelt Drive-In in Jersey City, New Jersey. (As it turned out, the character played by Walter Brennan recruits Leslie Nielsen's character to work with him in his advertising business.) Ruth and I dated for seven years. We decided to wait to get married until I had completed my two years in the Army and graduated from Fairleigh Dickinson University.

I worked for a couple of companies in New York City and New Jersey over the next nine years. Then one day I approached my wife with the idea of starting our own advertising and sales promotion business together. At that time, we had three young children and our finances were tight—we had only $600 in savings. If Ruth had expressed the least bit of doubt, I would not have taken the chance at the time. I am so grateful she loved the idea. She was very enthusiastic about it and had complete confidence we would succeed in our new venture.

I went to the bank soon afterwards and secured a 90-day loan for $5,000 to begin our business in one-third of the basement of our home in Landing, New Jersey. We purchased used office furniture for $95 and a typewriter from Kmart for $125. On June 1st, 1973, Jay R Associates (which later became Jay R Advertising) was born. Our goal at first was simple—to feed the kids! I went out on sales calls and Ruth handled all the office work. Fortunately, we secured orders from AT&T, IBM, Nabisco, and several pharmaceutical companies in the first three months, which enabled us to pay the loan back on time. We had a great deal of fun working together. One of our first orders was from a pharmaceutical company for a large quantity of four-inch tall rubber erasers in the form of a senior citizen named Minnie holding a sign that read, "Liberation from Constipation." (This was a tie-in to magazine ads the company was running at the time.) After this order, the company became a regular client, so to speak. I was surprised to discover that this eraser is memorialized as part of an online Museum of Kitsch! You can view a photo at awmok.com/?s=minnie.

Three years later, we moved to the nearby town of Succasunna. We upgraded our office space to a larger basement area in our new home. The business continued to grow as we added BASF, Johnson & Johnson, *The Wall Street Journal,* and *People* magazine to our list of clients. One memory that stands out is when I received a call from a potential customer who asked for help with a rush order. He needed a very specific kind of briefcase that he planned to present to a parting executive at a dinner the following evening. His regular vendors were not able to find it anywhere. With her magic touch and much research, Ruth managed to locate the company in Tennessee that manufactured it. We had the briefcase shipped overnight to our office and then I delivered it in person that afternoon. Within the year, that company become our largest customer.

Four years after that, we bought an office building on the main highway in town just two miles from our home. The business continued to grow and we eventually employed ten people. Space was getting tight, so we began looking into a bigger office space so we could hire more people. Just as we were ready to sign the contract for the new building, Ruth hesitated. She brought up the idea of selling the business instead and retiring while we were still young because, as she said, you never know what's going to happen. I initially hesitated, but after thinking it over, I knew she was right yet again—she was very insightful and had tremendous instincts all her life. Within three months, we sold our 14-year-old business to Robert Lieberman, president of All-Ways Advertising in Bloomfield, New Jersey. Jay R Advertising continues to this day these 48 years later as a division of Rob's company. (The new owner had to assign three full-time employees just to do Ruth's job.) We moved to Florida in 1990 and had a wonderful ten more years together. We spent this time with our children and grandchildren and did some traveling before Ruth passed away. She was only 58 years old.

I am thankful for my family (including my sons, Gary, Craig, and Jay; my sister, MaryLou; my sisters-in-law, Peg, Lucy, Pat, and Trudy; my daughters-in-law, Connie and Denise; and all my grandchildren and great-grandchildren), and my friends. I am grateful for the many good things I have experienced during my lifetime. I am looking forward to the years to come. As my Uncle Henry was fond of saying, "Everything is beautiful, right?" Though his question was rhetorical, I would still like to respond: Yes!

Thank you for reading my book. Comments are welcome. My email address is gacrja@aol.com. (*gacrja* comes from the first two letters of my sons' names.) I hope these cartoons make you laugh or smile. I'll even take groans—I'm not picky!

Jules Roma
Tequesta, Florida
May, 2021

P.S. Like father? Like son! If you are a fan of puns and a glutton for punishment, I highly recommend my son Gary's upcoming book, *Indelible Inklings: A Supersaturation of Puns* & *Pun Crystals: An Unforeseen Compilation.* (It is two-books-in-one. I think you will flip it over and flip over it!) Both his book and mine will be available for sale on his website, ironfrog.com, as well as at other outlets.

P.P.S. Here are some of Gary's puns:

What do you get when you cross a road with a bike?
To the other side.

A restaurant down the street serves hyena soup. It's the laughing stock of the neighborhood. When a critic wrote a review, he bit off more than he could eschew.

A kleptomaniacal baker *really* takes the cake.

I meant to bake some pumpernickel bread, but my plans went awry. (Sorry, I got a little caraway with that one.)

For a cooking class I'm taking, I wrote a paper on Romano cheese. It hasn't been grated yet.

Farmers have started planting cotton in Indiana. Now Muncie is the route of boll weevil. (More faithfully, *the grove of* Muncie is the route of boll weevil.)

What is the sauce of your information?

A First Online Date

I wore this disguise just in case you were my ex-wife!

I think I'll hop in the shower.

Lettuce Alone

Don't worry—it's chicken soup.

Counter Intelligence

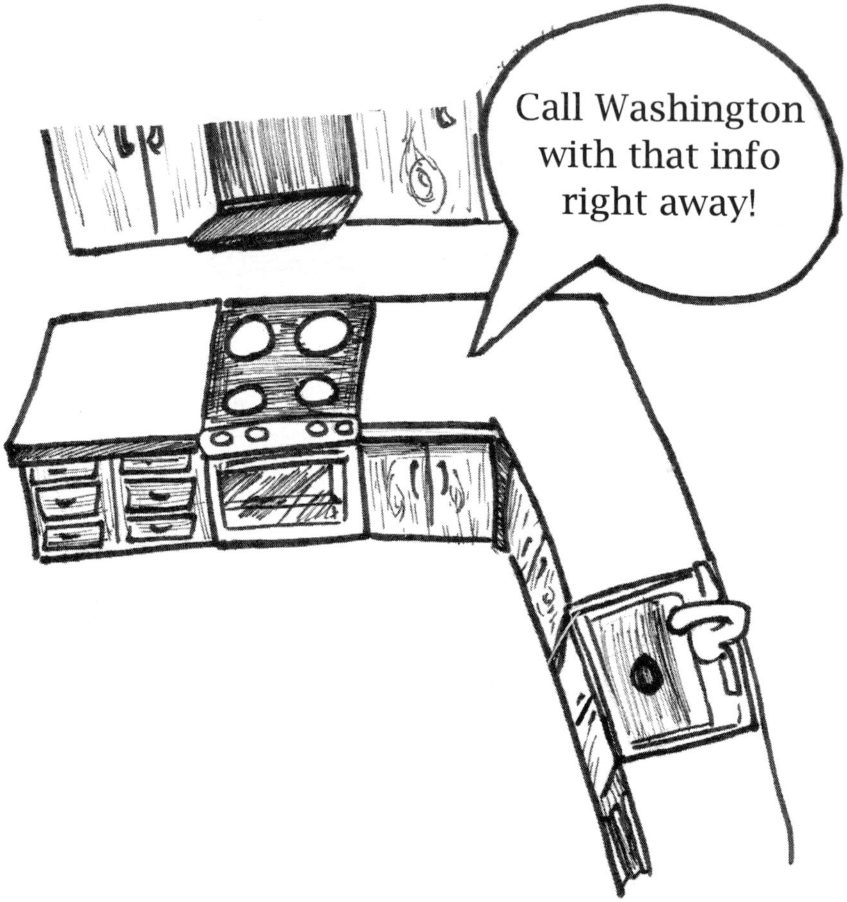
Call Washington with that info right away!

Pardon me, do you have any Grey Poupon?

I sure miss the good old days.

Mr. Wood, you are drifting again!

BUGABOO BAR
LADIES NIGHT

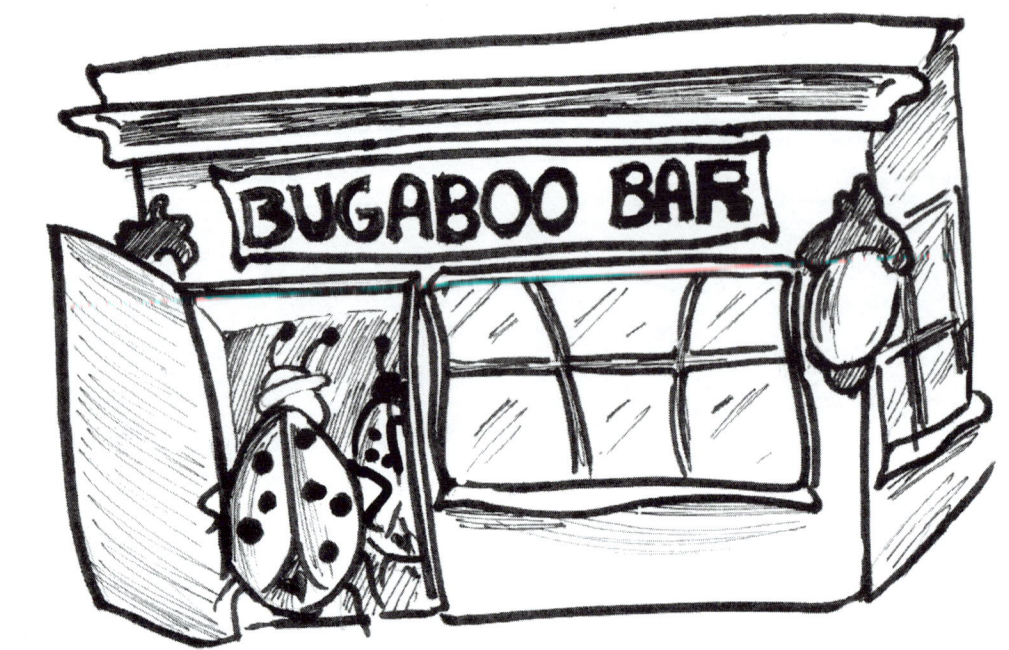

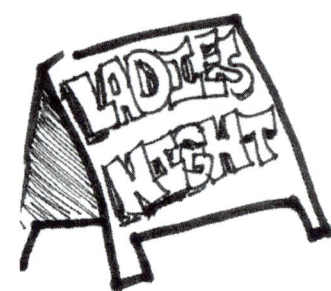

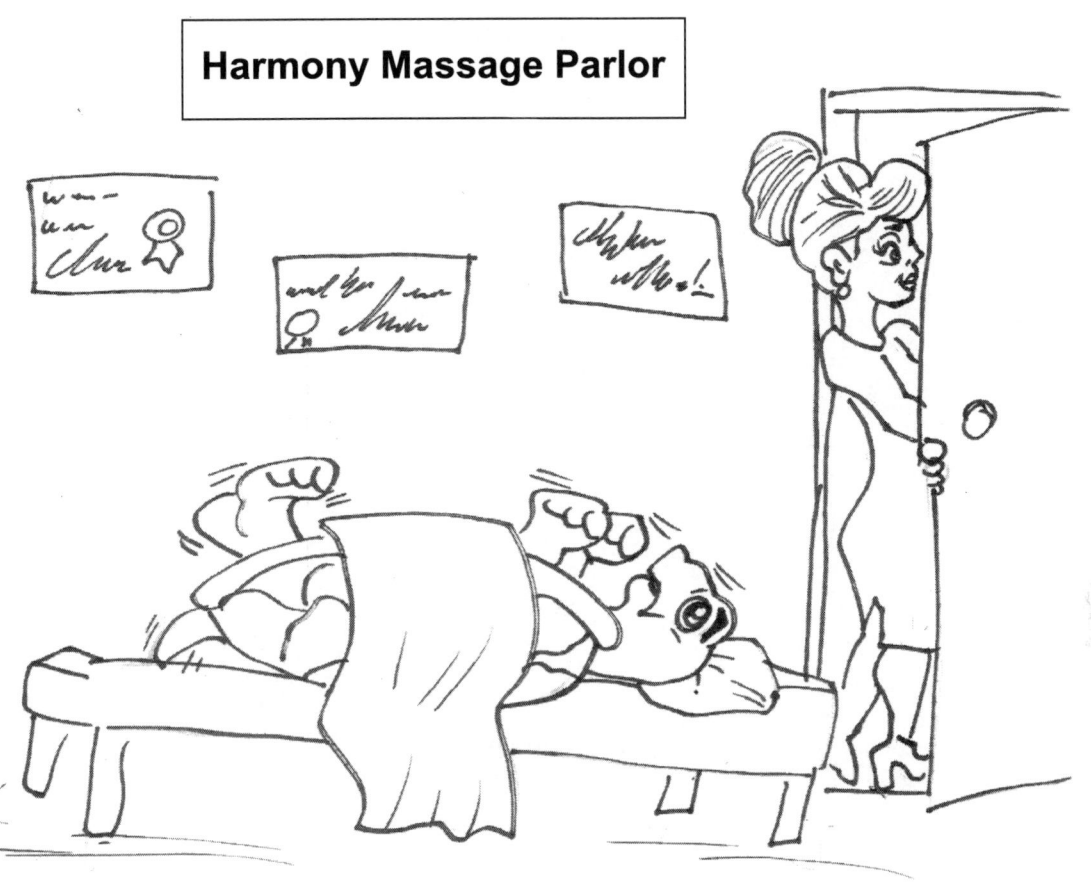

We're finished—you can get up now.

He has a big head since he became a kernel.

Oh wise man, what is the meaning of life?

Life is a cabaret, old chum.

These seeds taste good!

Follow me ... and make sure you're in a row.

I'm cold!

The Answer to an Age-Old Question

Just lay eggs.

Don't worry if the chicken or the egg came first.

It looks like rain dear.

Ever wonder what was in that mousehole?

There you go pigging out again!

Drop the bag—this is a stick-up!

Writer's Block

POLITICAL STATEMENT

Whatever it is, I've done nothing wrong.

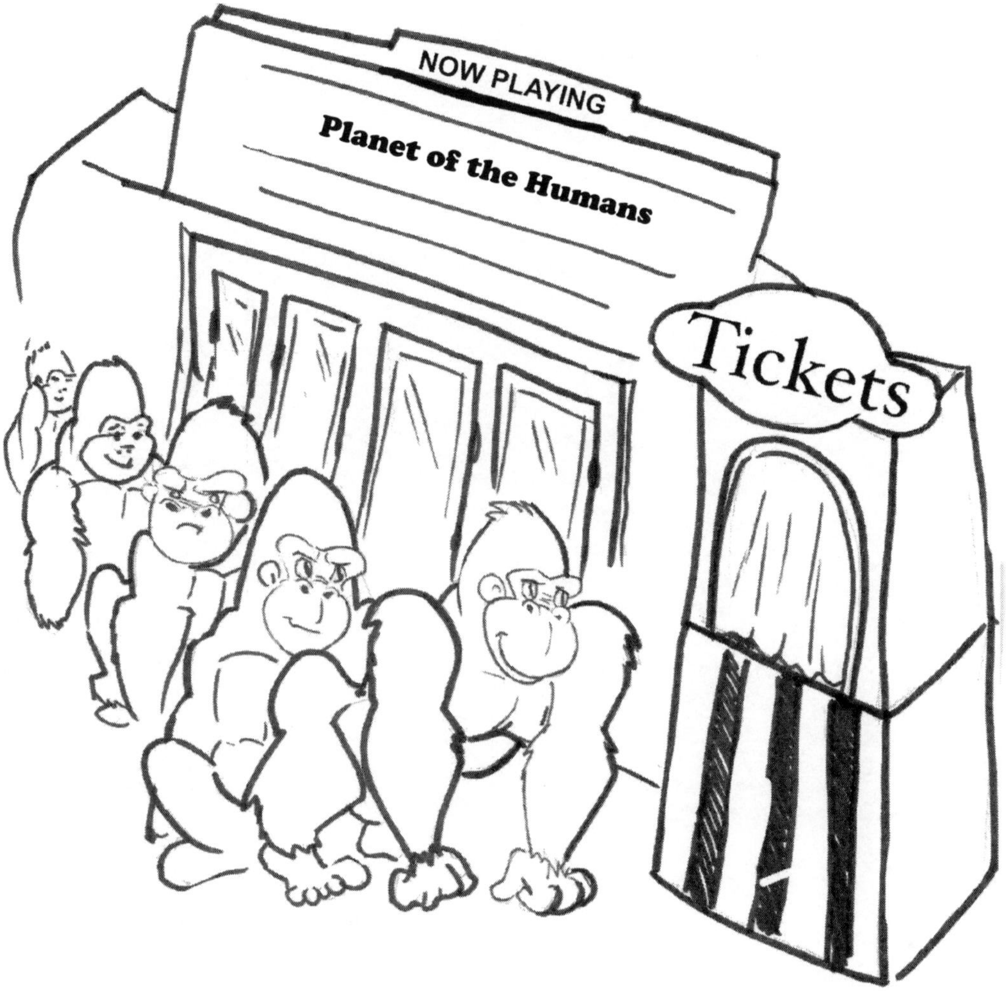
NOW PLAYING
Planet of the Humans
Tickets

It's okay to pee in the water.

I don't know—look it up in the phone book!

Dad, the computer is still on an online dating site.
I'll ask Mom for help.

Mom, look—Santa used the same kind of
wrapping paper that you bought at Walmart!

You never did measure up.

Don't let any pencils rub you the wrong way.

You're tuning me out.

That's not what I meant when I said I never have time for myself!

Who needs Florida? Three more months
and we will have sunshine.

Special Low Auto Insurance Rates For Teenagers

www.AreYouKiddingMe.com

It tastes like chicken!

We could always go live with our parents.

I'm afraid you have a very expensive ailment.

Moral—There is no accounting for taste.

I told you to use suntan lotion!

Dad, why do you keep calling it the Stupid Bowl?

What do you mean you can't find your camouflaged tank?

Hunting has been slow. Good thing we stocked up on Spam!

What smells?

Your new cologne is not working!

Don't act like we're humans. They'll think we're dumb.

It sounds like you're trying to make a monkey out of me!

How to Get Out of a Second Date

I've got to go.
One of my six children just locked the babysitter out of the house!

He said this is his most recent photo.

The Lone Ranger is one of our ancestors!

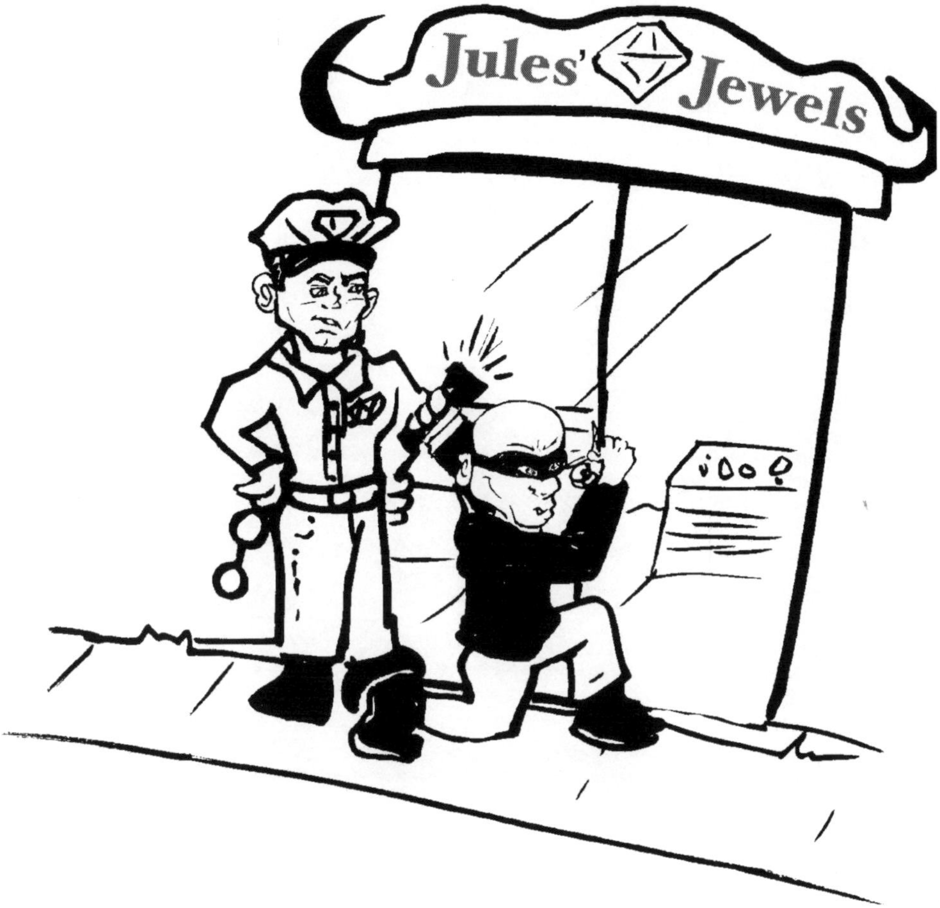
Jules' Jewels

Here—hold this.

House Wine

They will be tough to identify with those masks on.

Enlarged Prostate Social Club

I'm postdating this check six months.
We should be out of bankruptcy by then.

She is so appealing!

Ahhh, smooth, yet tangy, with good body.
Nothing like the 2020 Ripple!

How Milkshakes Were Invented

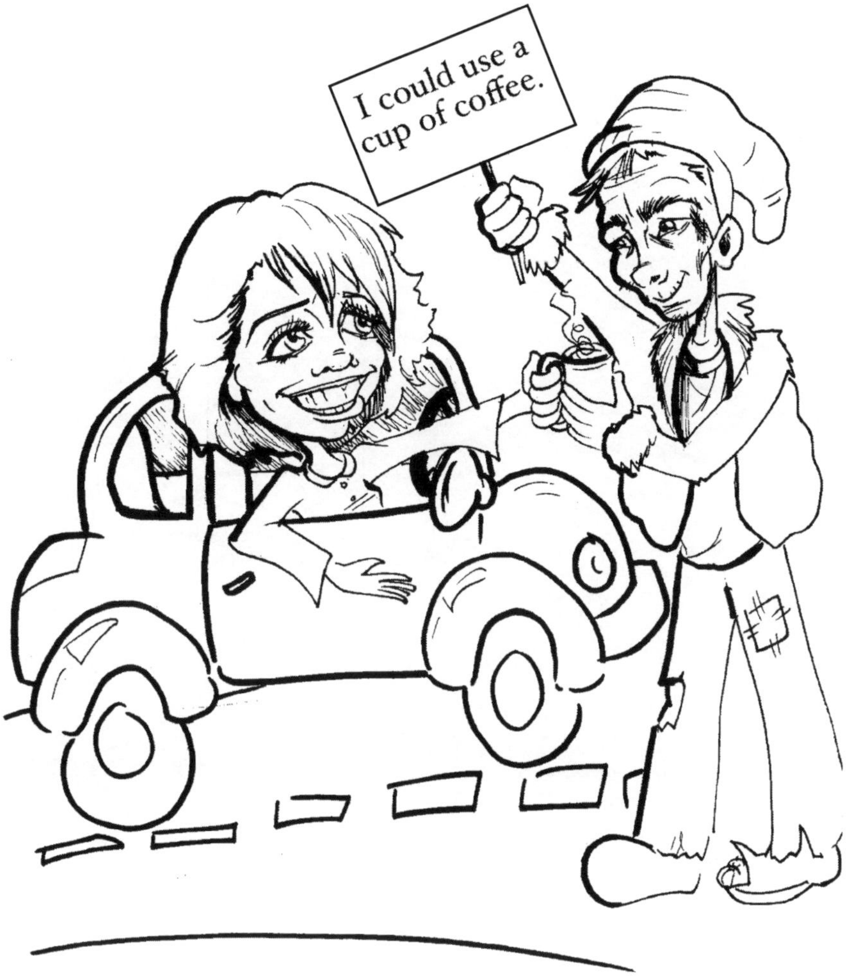
I could use a
cup of coffee.

Be careful.
Don't let any of those humans touch you—they'll give you warts!

Highway Robbery

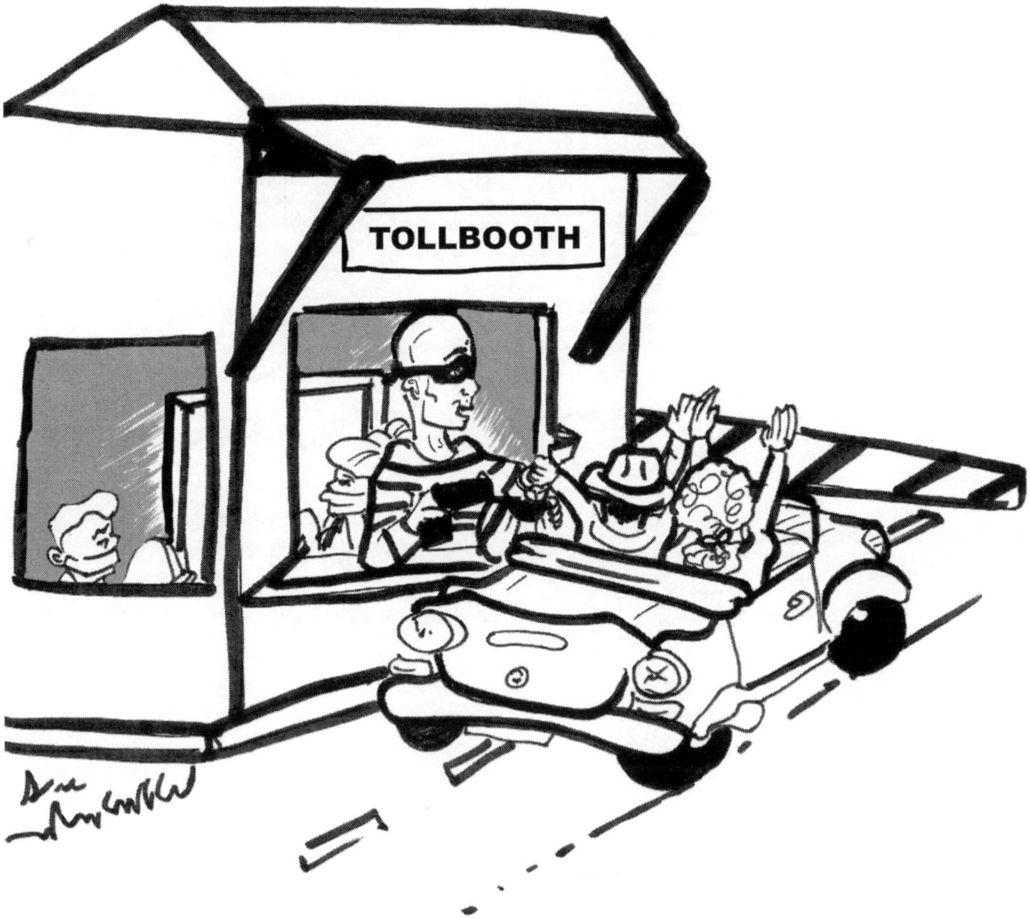
TOLLBOOTH

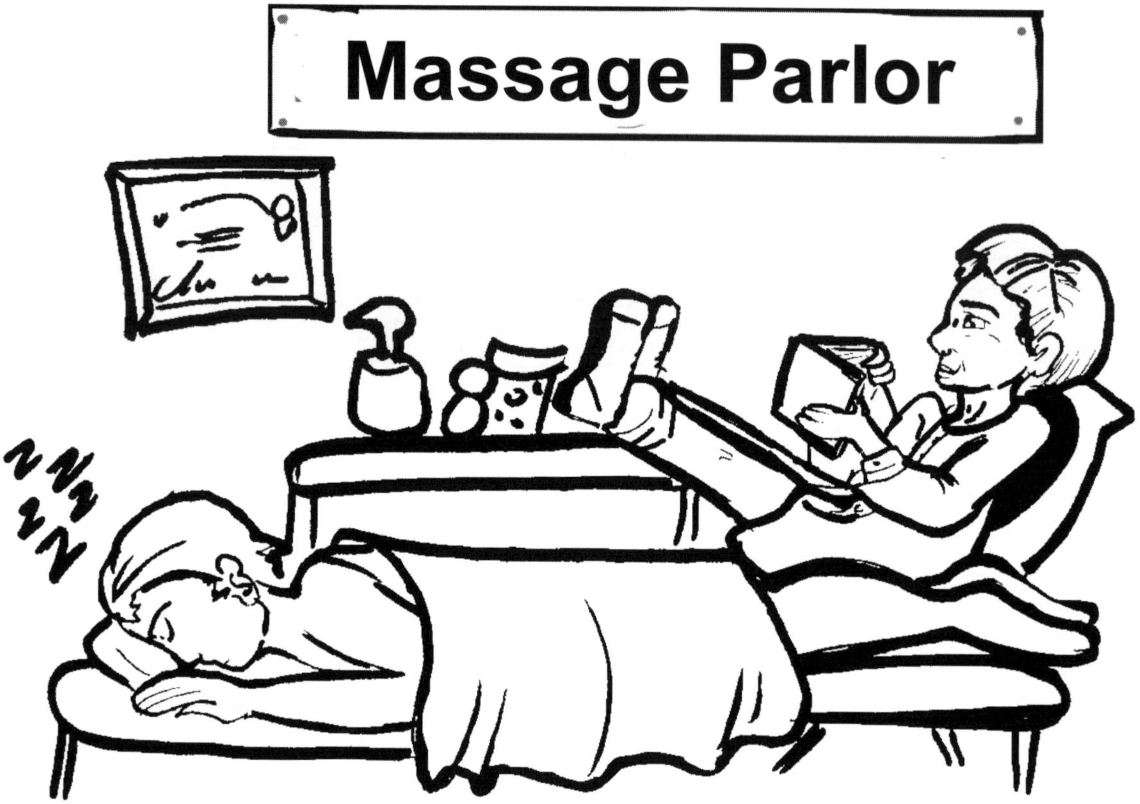
Massage Parlor
Z
Z
Z
Z
Z

They want us to perform.

Give them a raspberry and I'll hold my nose!

And remember, it's a jungle out there.

It's King Kong's brother, right?

Golf School

Remember—when you see that golf club coming towards you, veer to the right or left.

I see there is life on Mars!

But if we do what you say, I will go to jail!

That's okay, I'm a lawyer and I can defend you.

I told my boss I disagree ... and here I am.

Dad, you shouldn't suspend my allowance
just because you bought me two $12 hotdogs!

I told you to straighten up!

Senior Basketball Tournament

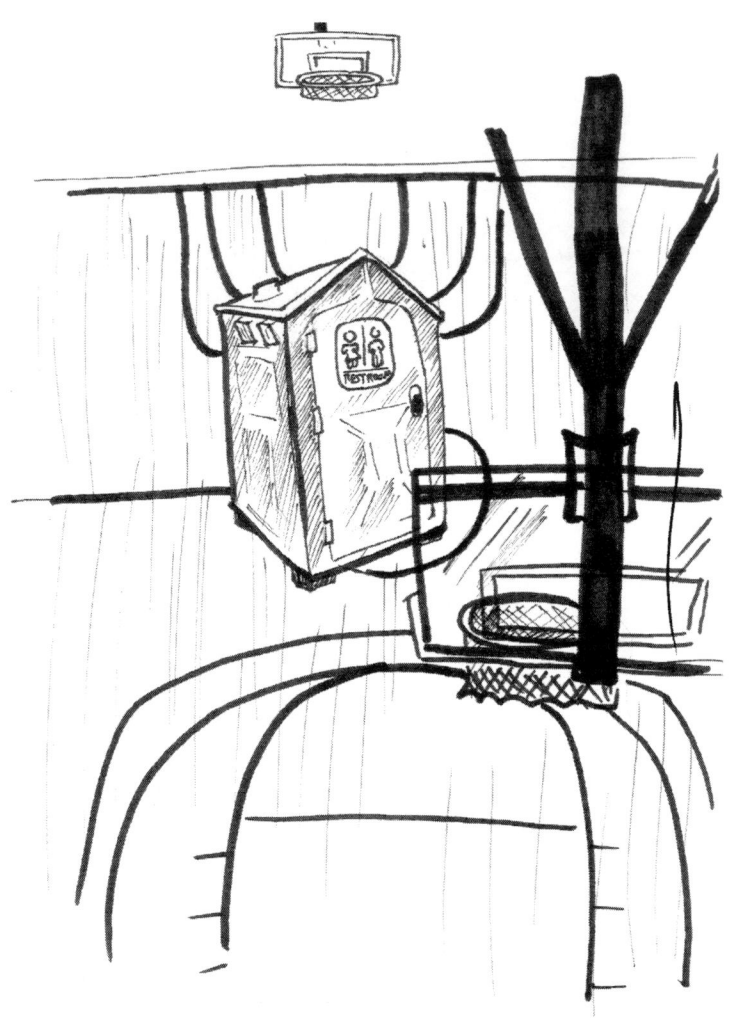

Wait here while I slip into something more comfortable.

I left my wife and said, "What now?"

Here Grandpa—it's fixed now!

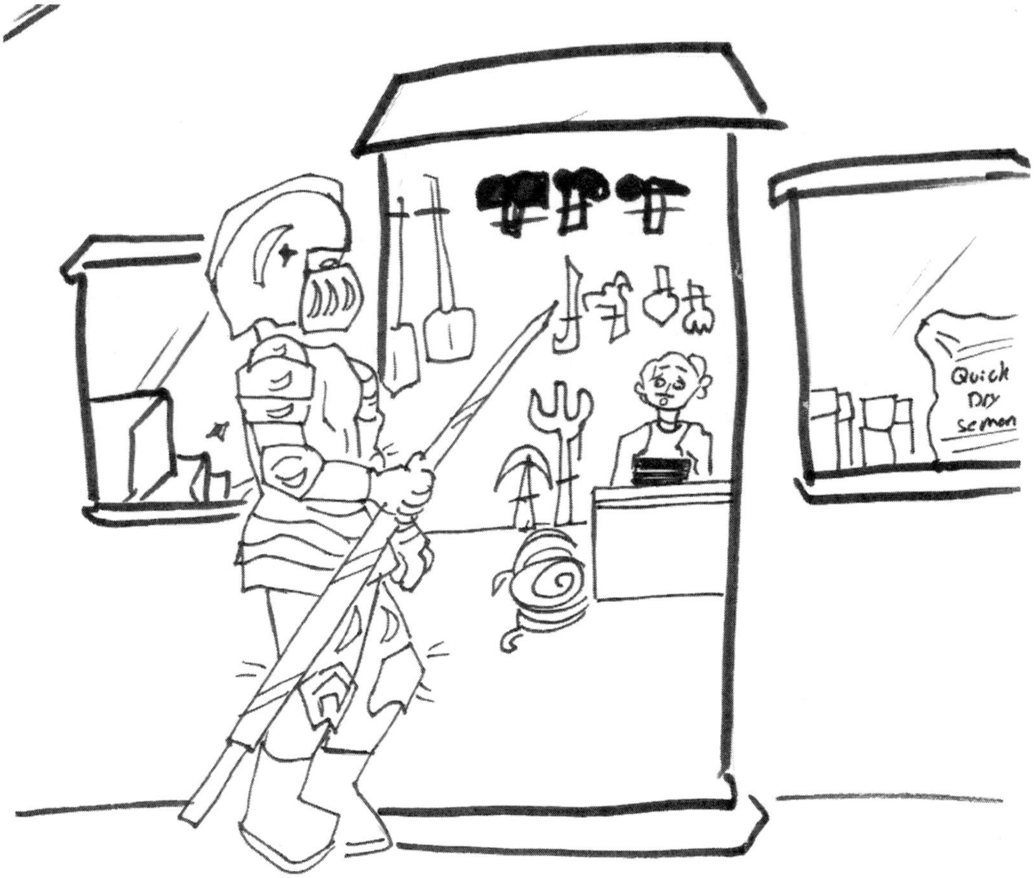
Quick
Dry
Semon

One can of WD-40, please.

Dear, it's very slow because it's not plugged in!

Golf Clinic Concussion Department

No homework tonight except to read the next four chapters.

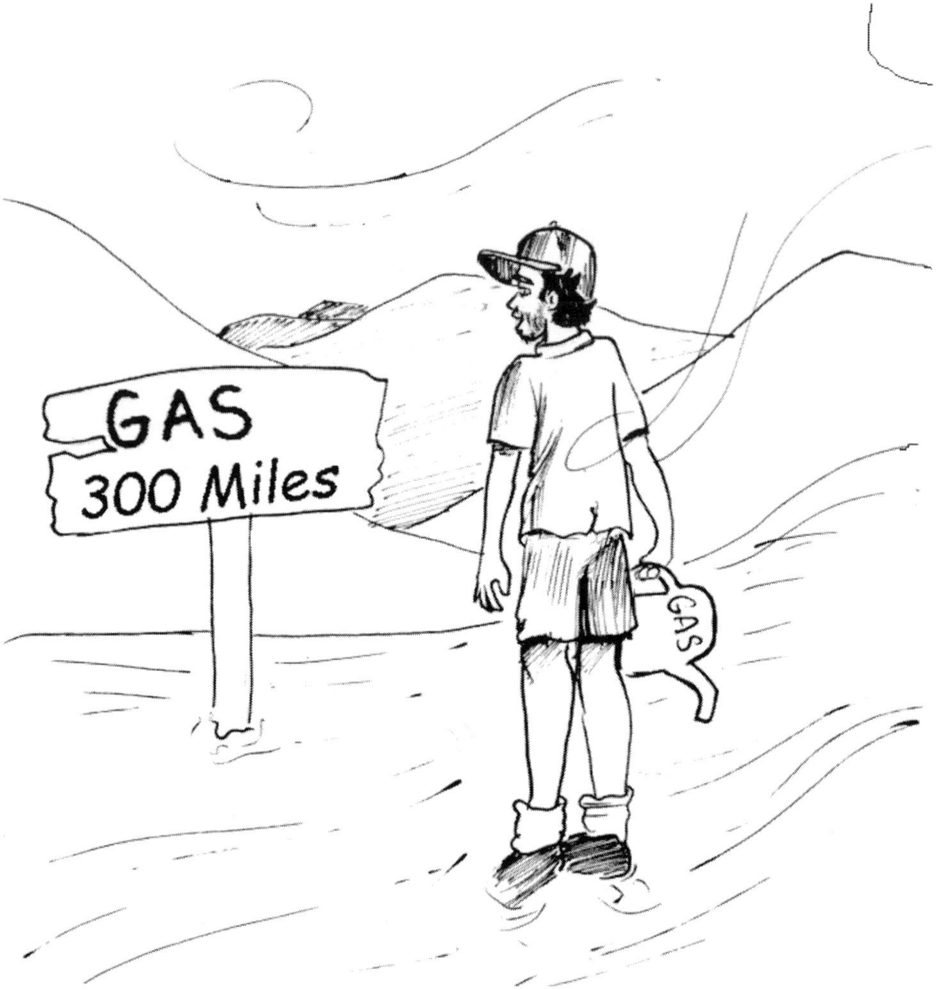
GAS
300 Miles
GAS

You should have your hearing checked.

I've come for you.
No, I've come for you.

Why do you want a divorce? Where would you live?
Who would you yell at?

Gorilla Warfare

I'm not getting older—I feel the same as last month.

Let's get back together—I can't find anyone else.

No, you can't claim an office in your home if you're unemployed.

I finally had a good online date last night.
It was with my ex-wife!

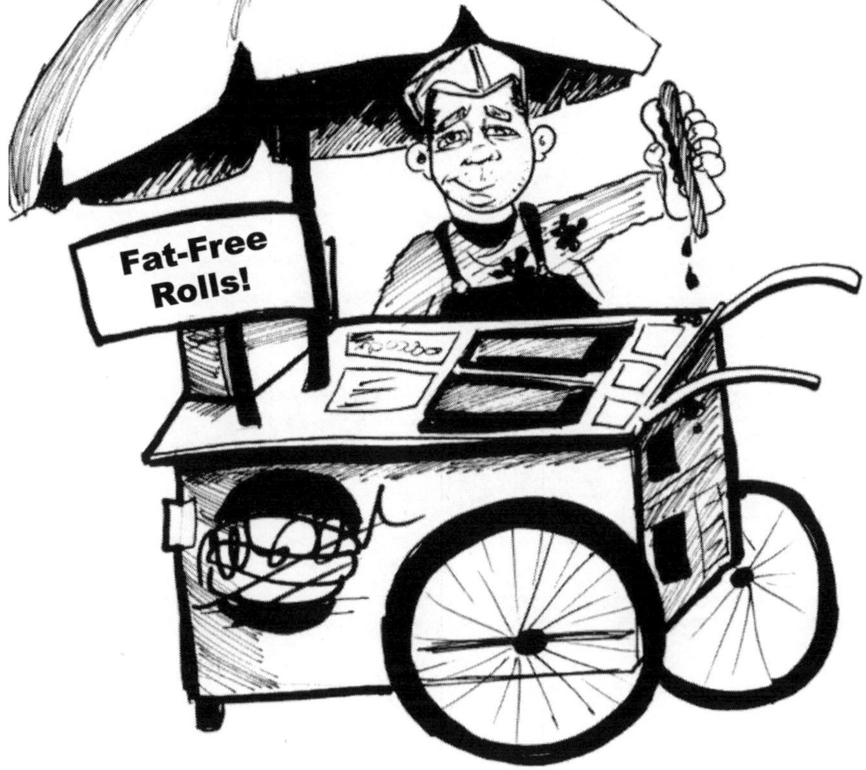
Fat-Free
Rolls!

The First Cell Phone

Great. More crumby food!

Yes, I love you. But I just can't stand being with you!

Since we're not engaged anymore, has enough time
gone by so I can hock the ring now?

I see your bird getting sick.

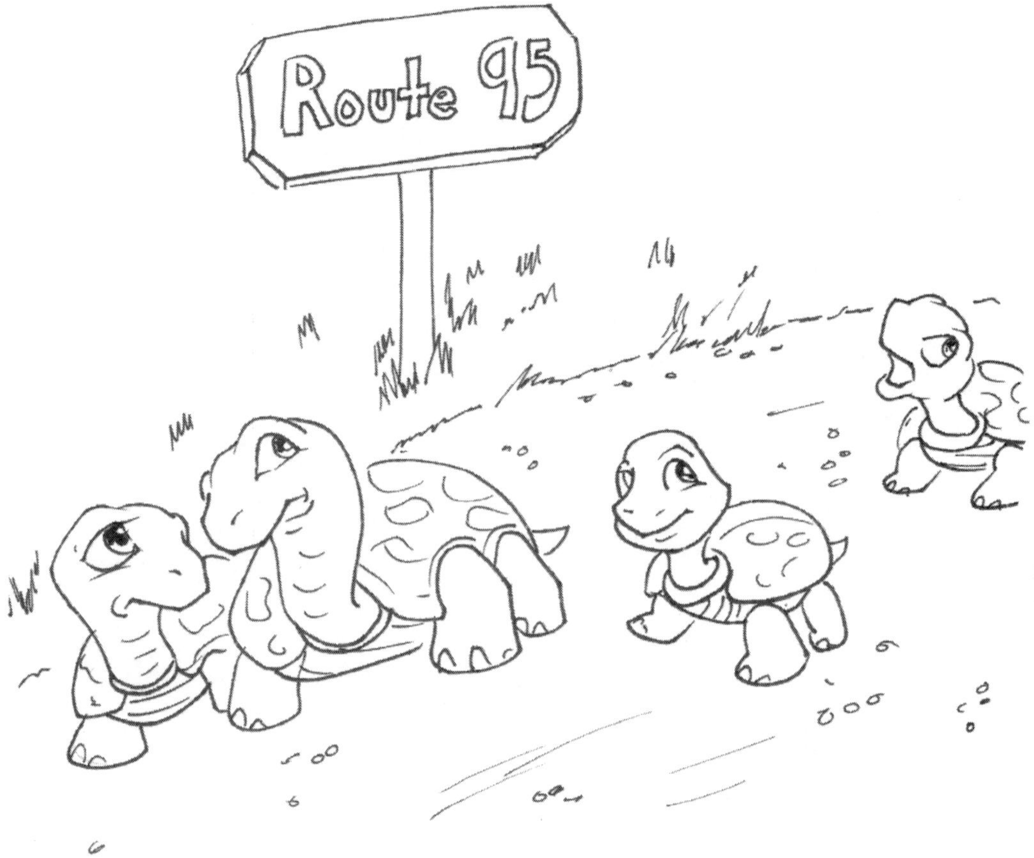
Route 95

Are we there yet?

I sure hope I don't have an enlarged prostate!

"I read this book and liked it," is not a book report!

How can I forget about it?

Thomas Edison

I'm out of ideas.

What a dumb game that is!

Gorilla Glue really works!

So you expect my blood pressure to be normal?

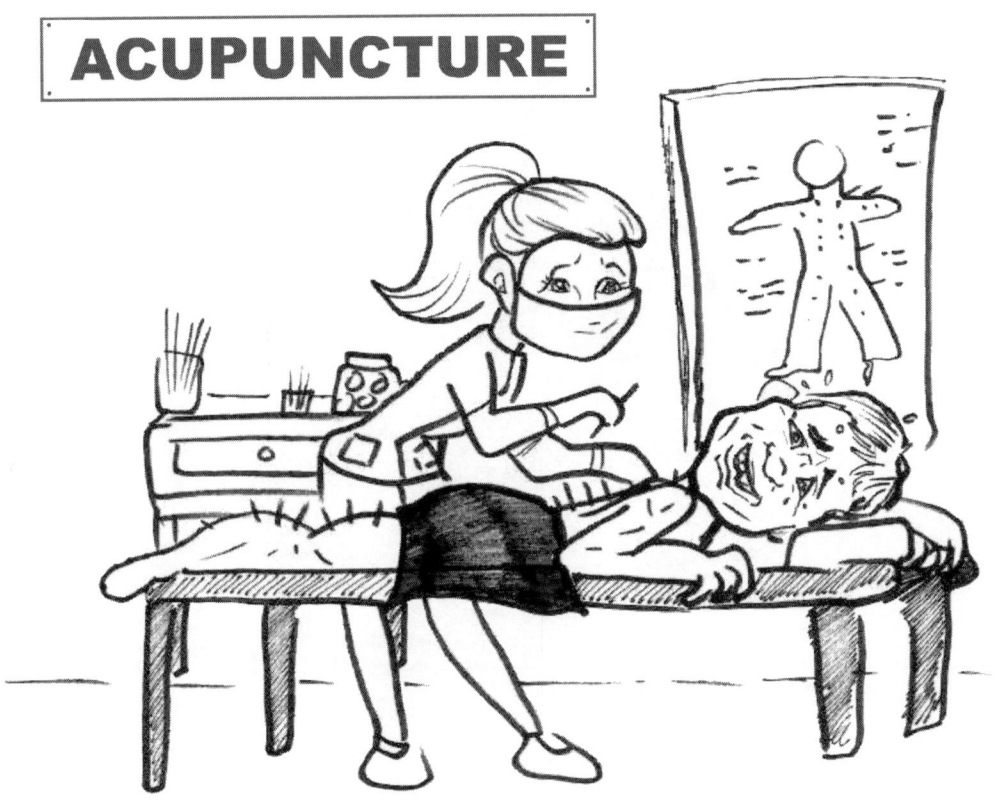

ACUPUNCTURE

Let me know when you are ready to start.

You didn't use your deodorant today.

Ma, these eggs are looking at me funny.

It's that darn dog again.

I'm sorry, sir. We can't take you without an appointment.

But *Donald* is such a common name.

Stop trying to butter me up.

You don't understand that I'm breaking up with you.
I better send you a text.

Why Alligator Tastes Like Chicken

I'll see your two lives and raise you three!

But dear, you don't have to go on a diet.

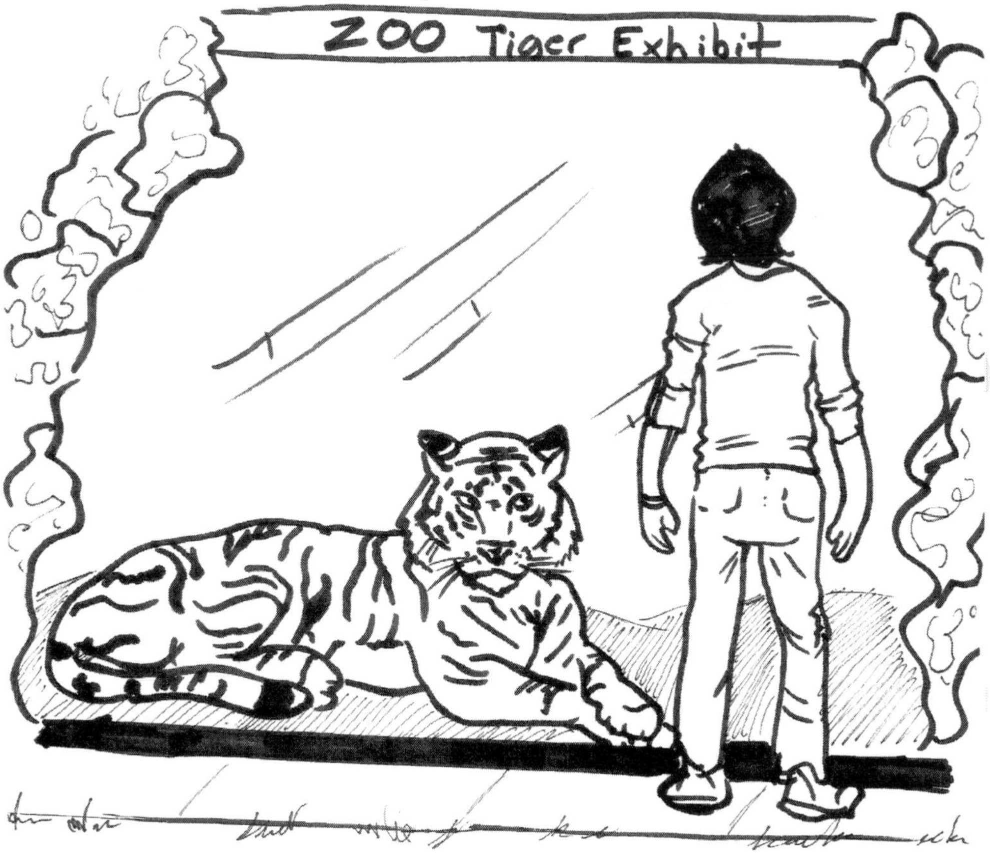
ZOO Tiger Exhibit

No, I'm not from Detroit.

I have the answer!

My blood pressure is normal now that
I stopped watching the news!

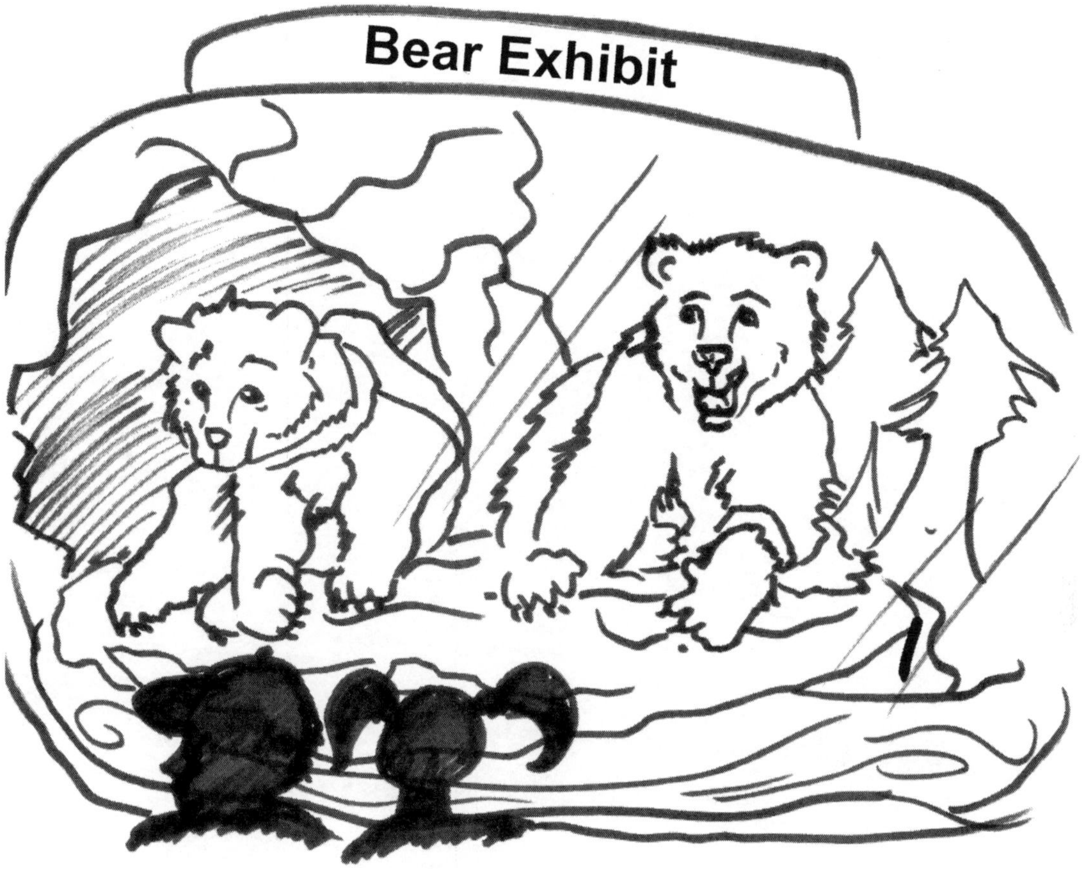
Bear Exhibit

I miss picnics.

Dear Diary, It was a beautiful day today.

Dear Diary, Nothing good happened today.

What do you mean you want a third set of books?

Sorry, we don't accept checks.

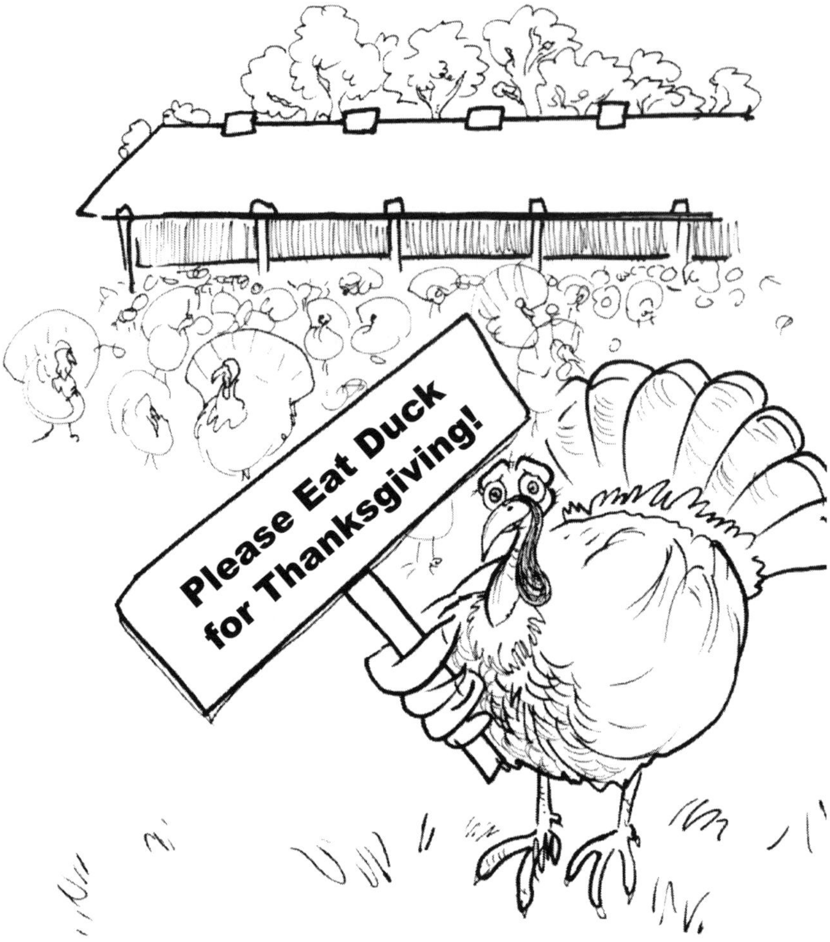
Please Eat Duck
for Thanksgiving!

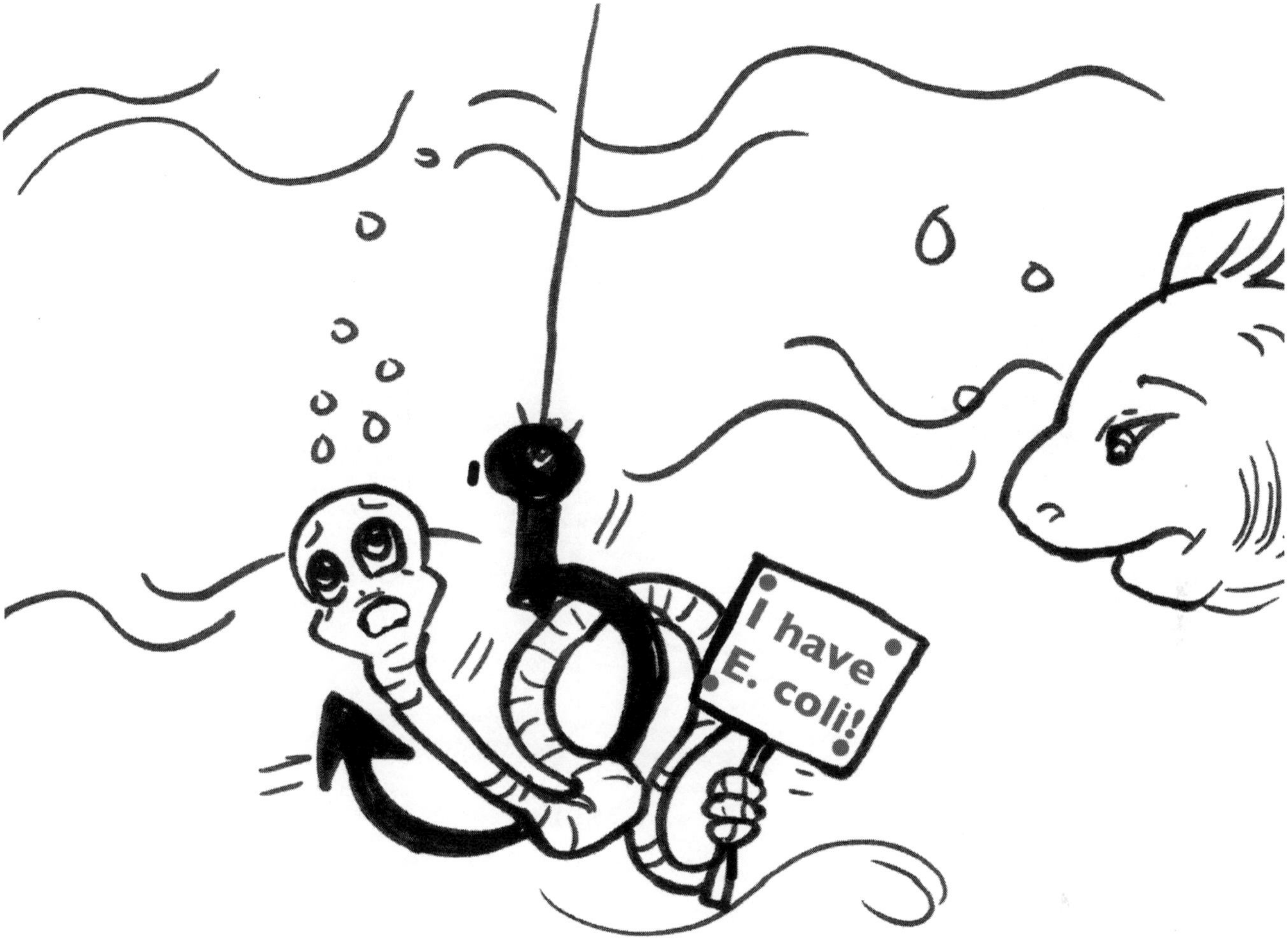
I have
E. coli!

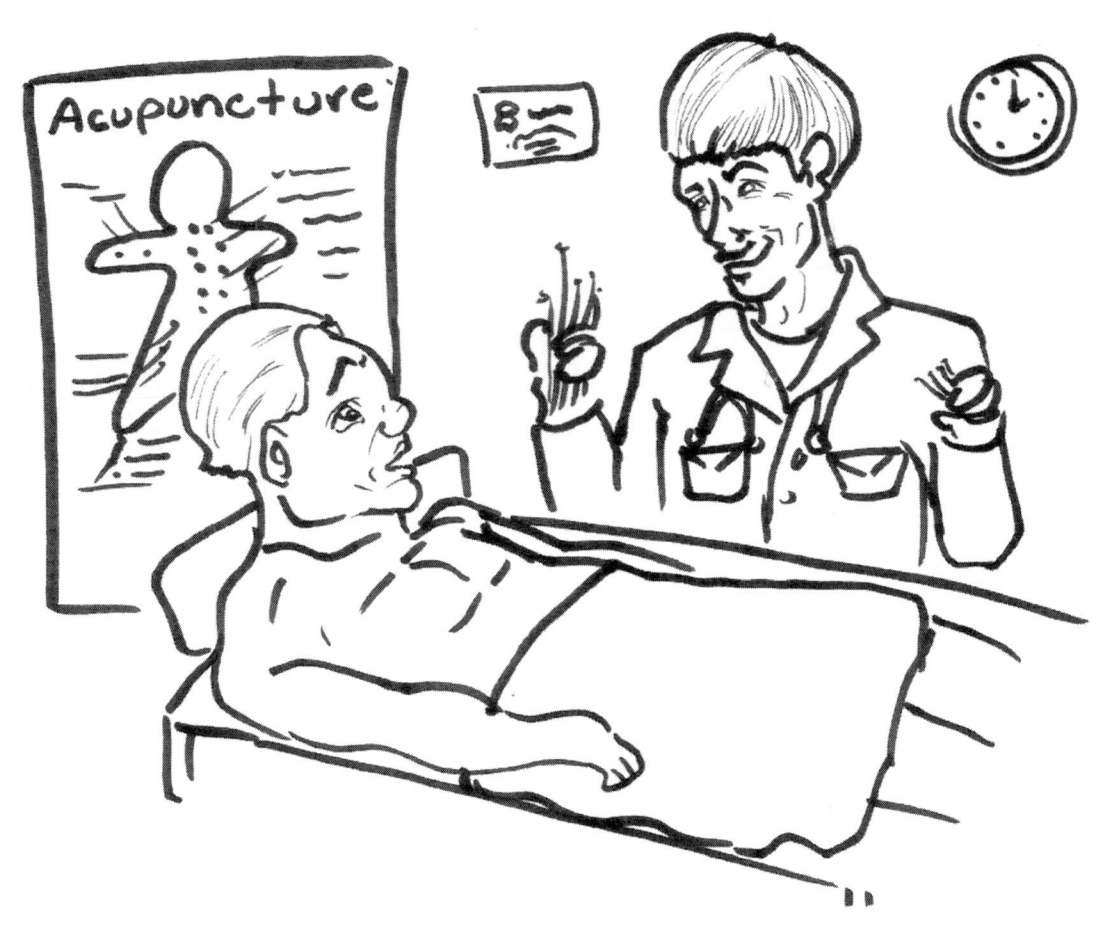

Are you a Democrat or a Republican?

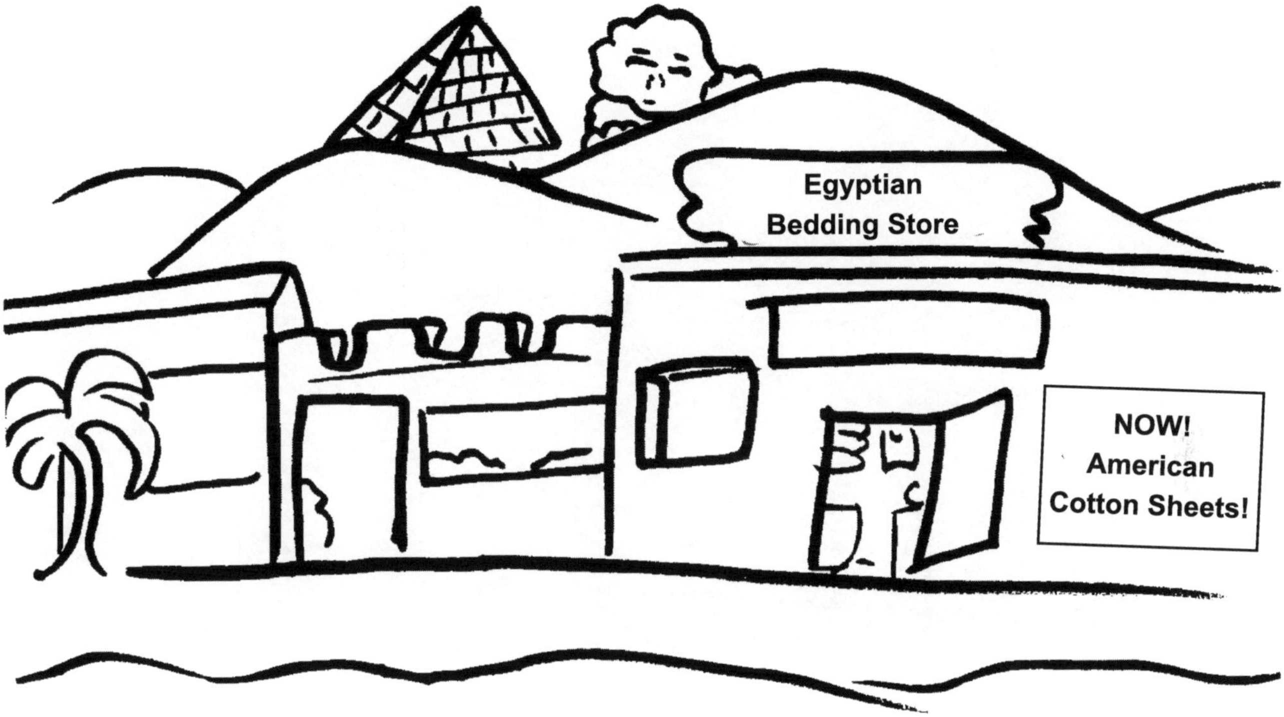
Egyptian
Bedding Store
NOW!
American
Cotton Sheets!

Ms. Smith, "This page left blank intentionally," should not be twelve pages of your book report.

Will you bear my children?

Give me 25 cents for the meter and I'll be right back.

What were we talking about? I forgot.

You must be Italian, Mr. Zucchini.

A Tie Restaurant

Classy Cuisine

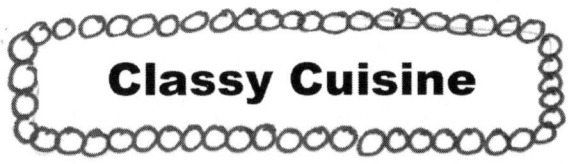

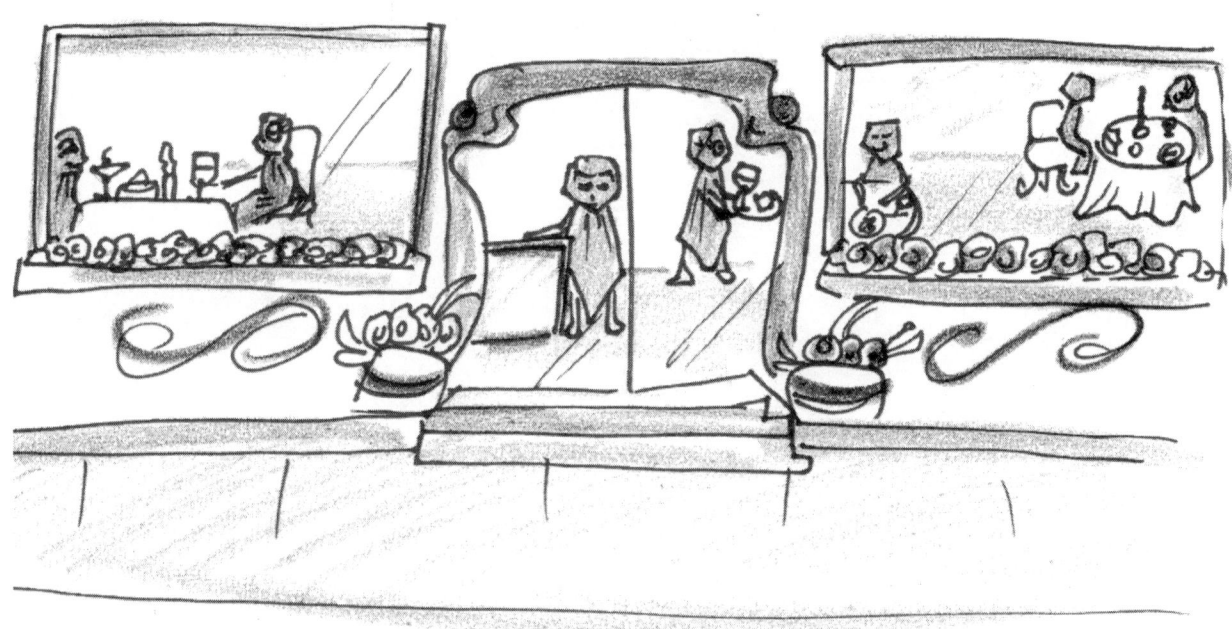

And to think, I gave up writing poetry for this!

At least I can eat faster than you.

Happy Valentine's Day!

Mutant Zebra

We need a new mouse.

The Father of Acupuncture

What's an app?

You got a problem with that?

It finally happened!

Remember when people trusted each other enough to
have their numbers printed in a public book?

Sorry, I forgot my keys!

A First Online Date

You look nothing like your photo on the dating site,
but I'll let you buy me dinner anyway.

A Recruit's First Night in the Army

What, no silk sheets?

I think I'm going to order a hamburger.

Cannibal!

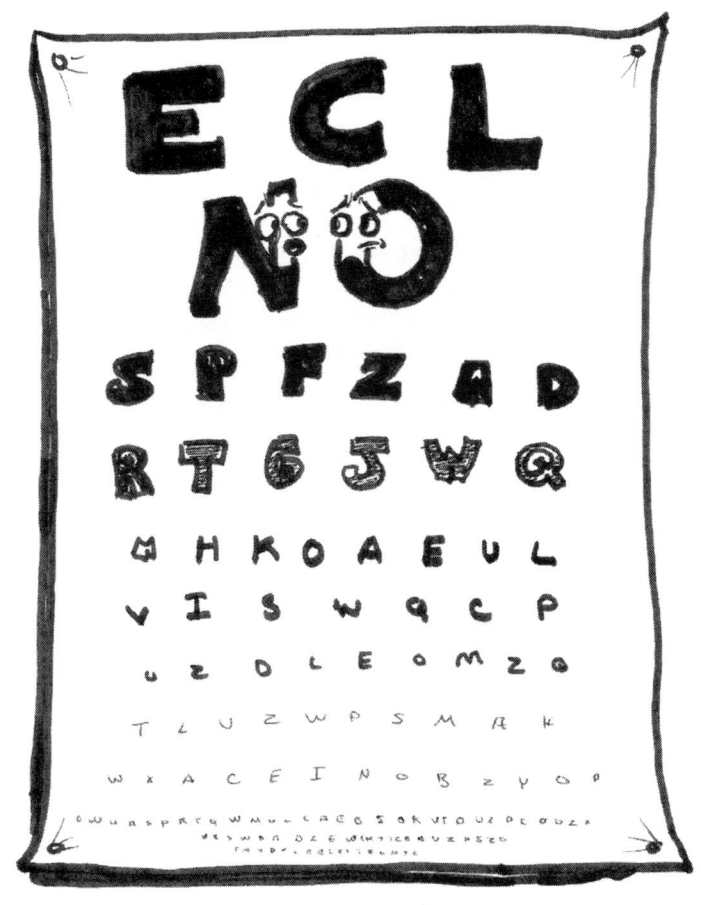

Quick, let's change places!

Oops! Only eight left.

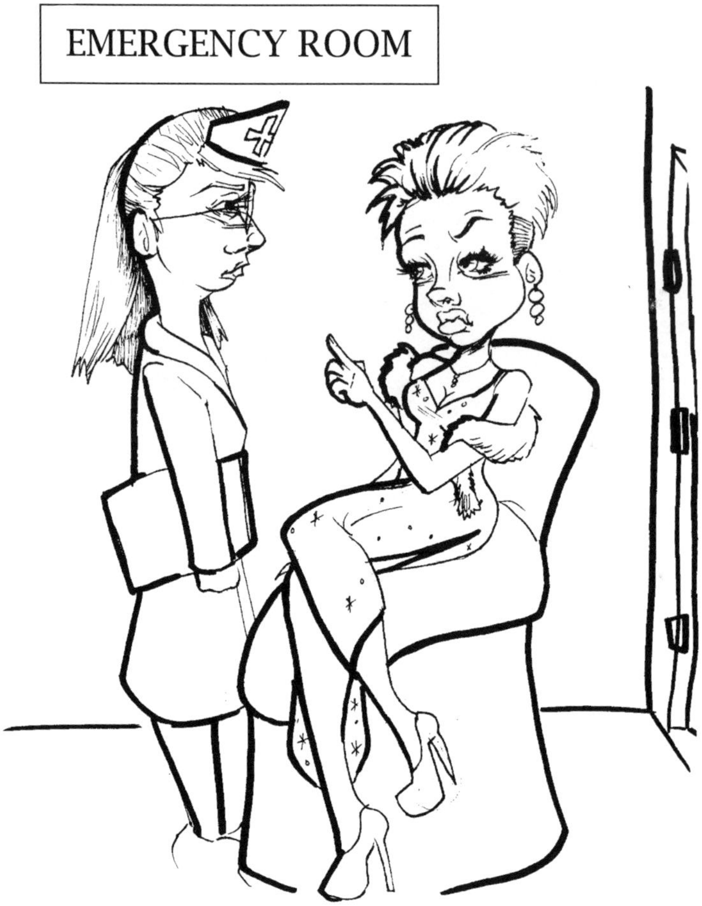
EMERGENCY ROOM

I have a splinter.

Darn cars with humans driving them!

I hope the furniture is okay.

Football

Bounced Checks

My alphabet is not finished because I had writer's block.

The Pen is Mightier than the Sword

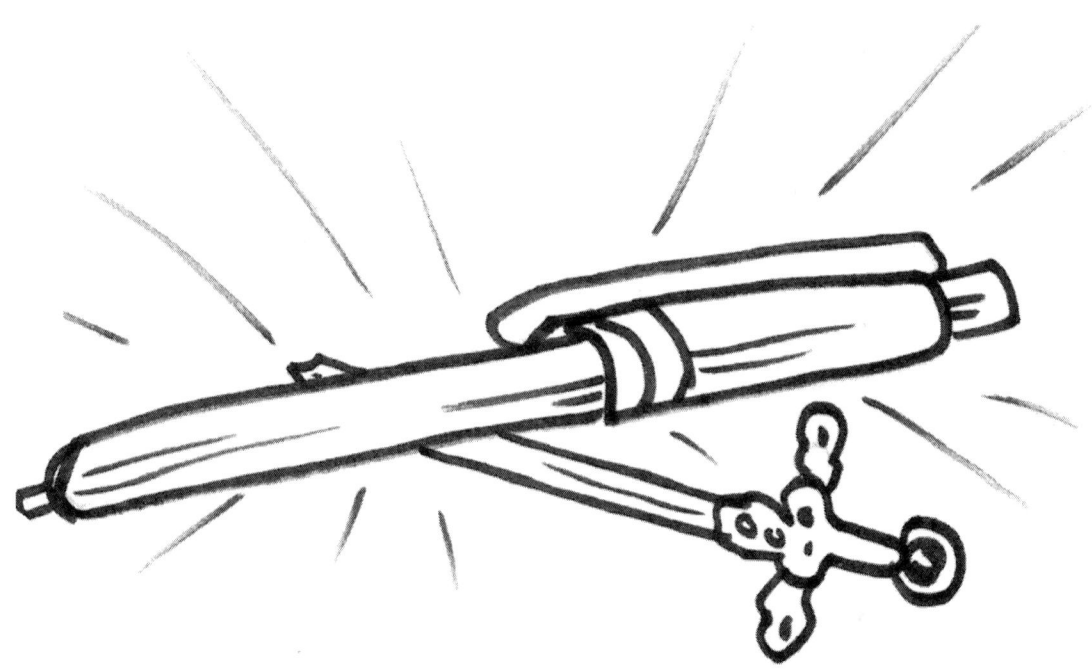

Looking for the love of my life.
The last twelve did not work out.

With the invention of the cell phone,
Superman has no place to change.

You're squashing me!

Thomas Edison

I've got an idea!

Some rich kid gave me almonds instead of peanuts!

Thank goodness they wear orange vests—it's easier to spot them.

Well, last year it was *fake!*

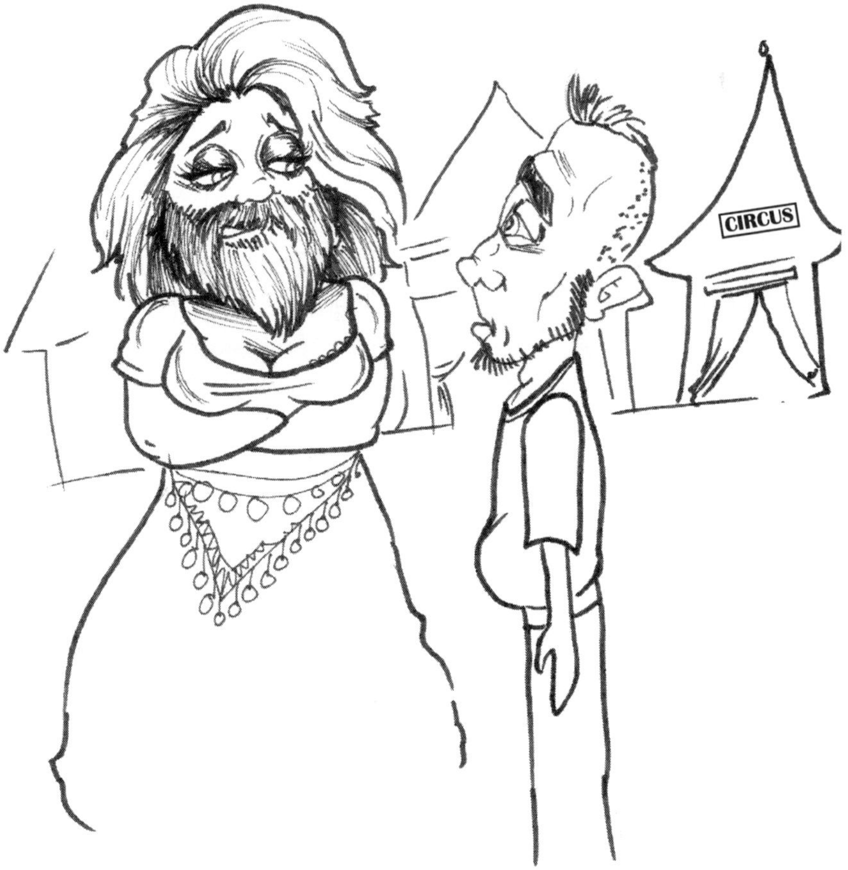
CIRCUS

Sorry, but I prefer clean-shaven men.

I see you're losing your hair. Stay out of the wind!

You seem really crabby today.

Zebra in Jail

Horseshoe Crabs Playing Horseshoes